Mia and Anthony and the Hidden Treasures

Treasure Number Three –
Our Very Special Family

About the Author

Joe Khoury writes on topics that are important to him; on core values that he hopes would inspire, educate and enlighten his children, step-children and hopefully others.

In 2019 he found a few precious notes in his mother's handwriting; Having lost both his parents while so young, he realized that he didn't really know much about them: what were their likes, dislikes, hopes, fears and even points of view on certain topics? He decided to begin writing so that – in the event that something should happen to him, my children and even future grandchildren would be able to know the core values and life lessons he hopes for them to learn.

Learn more about the author and the characters by visiting our website at
lessonsformykidsbooks.com
or scan the QR Code below

The house filled with noise as Anthony and Mia came charging downstairs.

"Hurrah! Today's our school trip to the museum! Where are my shoes, Mom?" shouted Mia. "What's for breakfast?" asked Anthony. "Let's eat quickly and get going. I don't want to be

late for the trip."

"I can't find my schoolbag," moaned Mia

"There's no juice in the fridge," complained Anthony. "Good morning, children," said Dad.

"Did you sleep well?" asked Mom.

"Mom, I can't find my new coat," said Mia. "I want to wear it for the trip." "Dad, can we go to the park later?" asked Anthony.

"I said, 'Good morning,'" replied Dad, slowly. The children looked at Dad.

"Erm… Good morning, Dad. Good morning, Mom," said Anthony. "Hello Mom, hello Dad," said Mia. "Erm… How are you?" "That's better," said Mom.

"Why?" asked Anthony. "We see you every day, so we don't need to say 'Hello' every time.

Anyway, I'm hungry. What's for breakfast?"

"Anthony!" said Dad. "How do you think me and Mom feel when you run in shouting for things?"

Anthony and Mia looked at each other. They were very good children most of the time, but they knew they'd done something wrong.

"Sorry," they both said.

"I don't understand, though," said Mia. "You're our family. So, why should we bother being polite?"

"Good morning, Mia and Anthony," said Jillian, coming into the room. "Here you are, Mia, I've found your shoes."

"Good morning, you two. Here's your coat, Mia," said Joanna.

"Thank you," said Mia, smiling. Her big sisters were always so helpful.

"How do you think we got this?" Mom asked, holding up Mia's lovely, new coat. "We bought it at the store," replied Mia.

"Yes, but first somebody designed it, then somebody made it, then somebody took it to the store and then somebody sold it.... and all those people worked together so you could have your coat."

"I don't understand," said Mia.

"Well, if people have to work together just to make a nice coat, think how much work is needed to make a nice family."

The children sat down to breakfast while Mom and Dad talked. "So, tomorrow isn't the best day, then?" Mom asked Dad.

"Not really," said Dad. "I have work to do. Sunday morning is fine, though" "Hmm," said Mom. "But we're going to church on Sunday morning." "What about Sunday afternoon, then?" asked Dad.

"That might work," replied Mom. "I'll check with Dominick, in case he is doing something on Sunday."

"Yes," said Dad. "I've already asked Jillian and Joanna, and I'll speak with Deanna later. It's tricky finding a time to suit everyone."

"Why are you both always talking and planning things?" asked Anthony.

"Well," said Dad. "We're a big family, so we need to make sure our plans work for everybody, don't we?"

"Why?"

"Well, how would you like it if we organized a big family party or a fun trip to the zoo when you were at school?"

"Don't you dare!" laughed Mia.

The twins were so excited about their trip to the museum that they forgot to ask Mom and Dad what they were planning for Sunday afternoon. After Mom had made breakfast and helped Mia find her schoolbag, they left for school.

Anthony and Mia were very excited when they arrived at the museum with their school friends. The teacher told the children to be careful. Everybody had to follow the museum's three golden rules. These were:

DON'T TOUCH ANYTHING

NO RUNNING

NO SHOUTING

At first, everything went well, and the children enjoyed looking around.

But then...

"I bet you can't catch me!" shouted one of their friends and ran off. Soon, all the children were running around. Anthony and Mia didn't want to break the rules, but their friends kept asking them to join in the game.

As soon as they did, something awful happened. Anthony tripped, and Mia crashed into him.

They both fell over and knocked over a vase.

CRASH!!

That was the end of the museum trip.

When they arrived home after school, Mom and Dad wanted to hear all about the museum. "What was it like?" asked Dad.

Mia said nothing and looked down.

"Um… can we go to the park?" replied Anthony

"Did something happen?" asked Mom. She knew something was wrong.

"No!" the twins yelled at the same time. Mom and Dad looked at them and waited. The twins began to cry.

"if something's wrong, we can only help if you tell us about it," Dad told them.

So the twins told Mom and Dad all about the accident. Jillian and Joanna came in to listen, followed by Deanna and Dominick.

"Well," said Dad, after they'd finished. "That was bad, wasn't it?"

"Don't you love us anymore?" asked Mia sobbing.

"Don't be silly," said Mom. "Of course we do. We're your family." "Families always love each other, whatever happens," said Dad.

"Yes," said Jillian.

"We all made mistakes when we were your age," said Joanna. "And we still make them," said Deanna.

"And we all still love each other," said Dominick.

"You see," said Mom. "We talk, and we help each other, and we are always, always there for each other."

"Even when we're naughty?" asked Anthony.

"Yes," said Dad. "You're always safe at home. It's where we share our problems so we can fix them."

"How?" asked Mia.

"Well, I'll go to the museum tomorrow and speak to the manager. You can come with me because it's Saturday and there's no school."

"I don't want to go back there," said Anthony. "I don't either," said Mia.

"Well, I'd love to go," said Dominick. "So would I," said Deanna.

"We want to come," added Jillian. "We haven't been to the museum for ages, have we, Joanna?"

The next day, the whole family went to the museum. The man at the museum was really pleased to see everybody and told the twins how nice they were to come and say sorry.

"I'm glad we told everyone what happened," said Anthony. "Yes," said Mia. "We'd still be worried if we didn't."

"And you'll be able to come back to the museum again, now," said Joanna. "Look! There's a cool exhibition about dinosaurs next week. Shall I take you to it?"

"Yes, please!" grinned Anthony. "I love dinosaurs!"

"I'll draw you the best dinosaur picture, ever, Joanna!" shouted Mia. "Thank you," said Joanna. "It's nice to do things for each other, isn't it?"

"Yes," added Dominick. "If we're kind, we'll always be a strong and loving family."

"You're right!" called Anthony. "I'll draw a dinosaur picture for you, as well." Dominick smiled and gave Anthony a big hug.

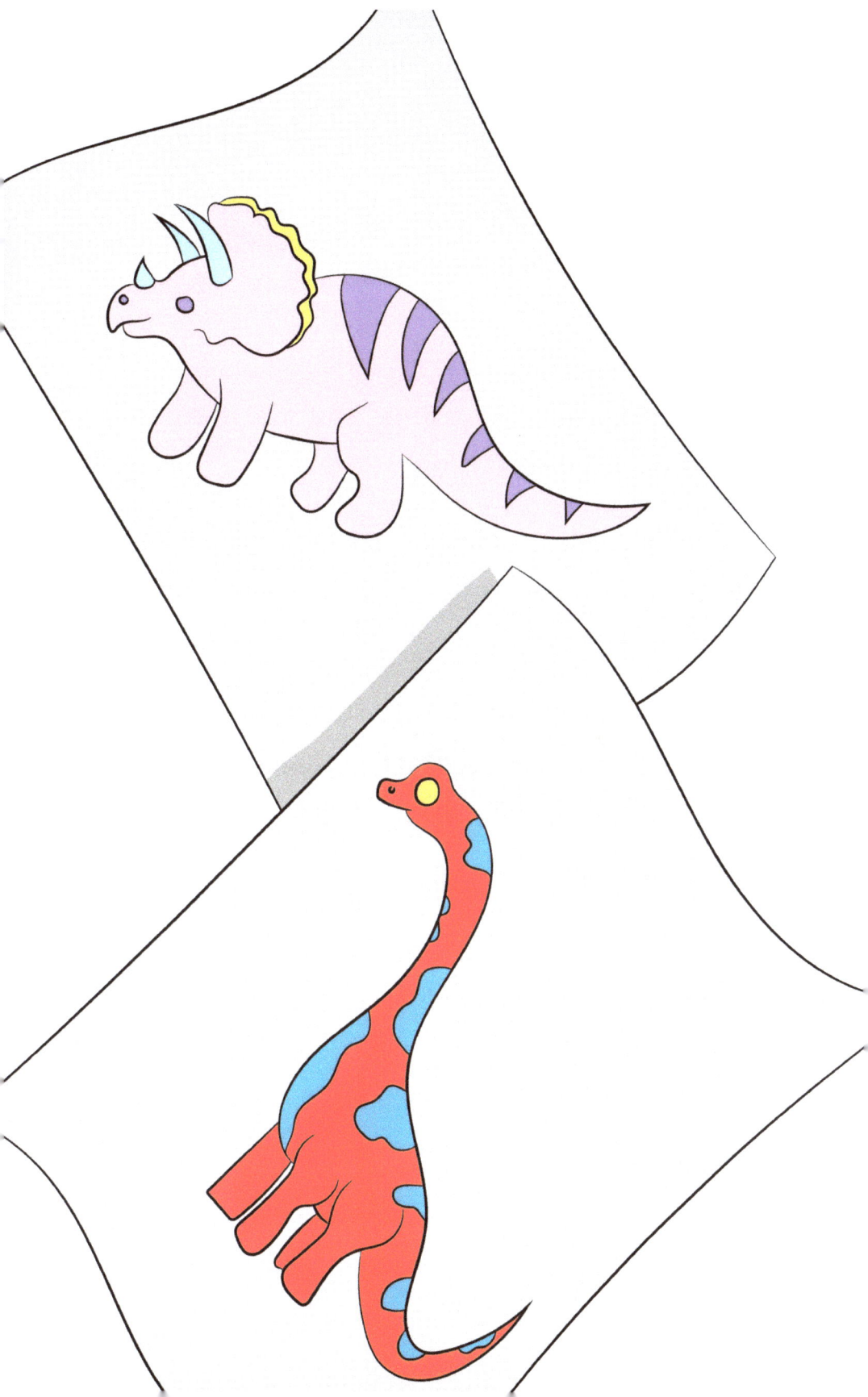

As they arrived home, the mailman walked towards them.

"Well, there are quite a few packages for you, today," he said. "One… Two… Three… Four… There you go."

What an exciting surprise! The family hurried inside and started opening the packages. The first package was for Dominick.

"It's from Grandma Gil!" he cried. "Wow! It's a really cool shirt. Look!" Dominick held up his gift so everyone could see it.

"I've got a new sweater," said Deanna.

"Good! Now, you can stop borrowing mine without asking," said Joanna. "I don't like your silly, old sweater, anyway," replied Deanna.

"Now, now, girls," interrupted Mom. "Don't argue."

Joanna and Deanna smiled at each other. They were sisters and didn't want to fall out through a silly argument.

"Grandma has sent me that book I wanted," said Joanna as she opened her package. "And she's sent me a DVD," said Jillian. I hope I can find the DVD player.

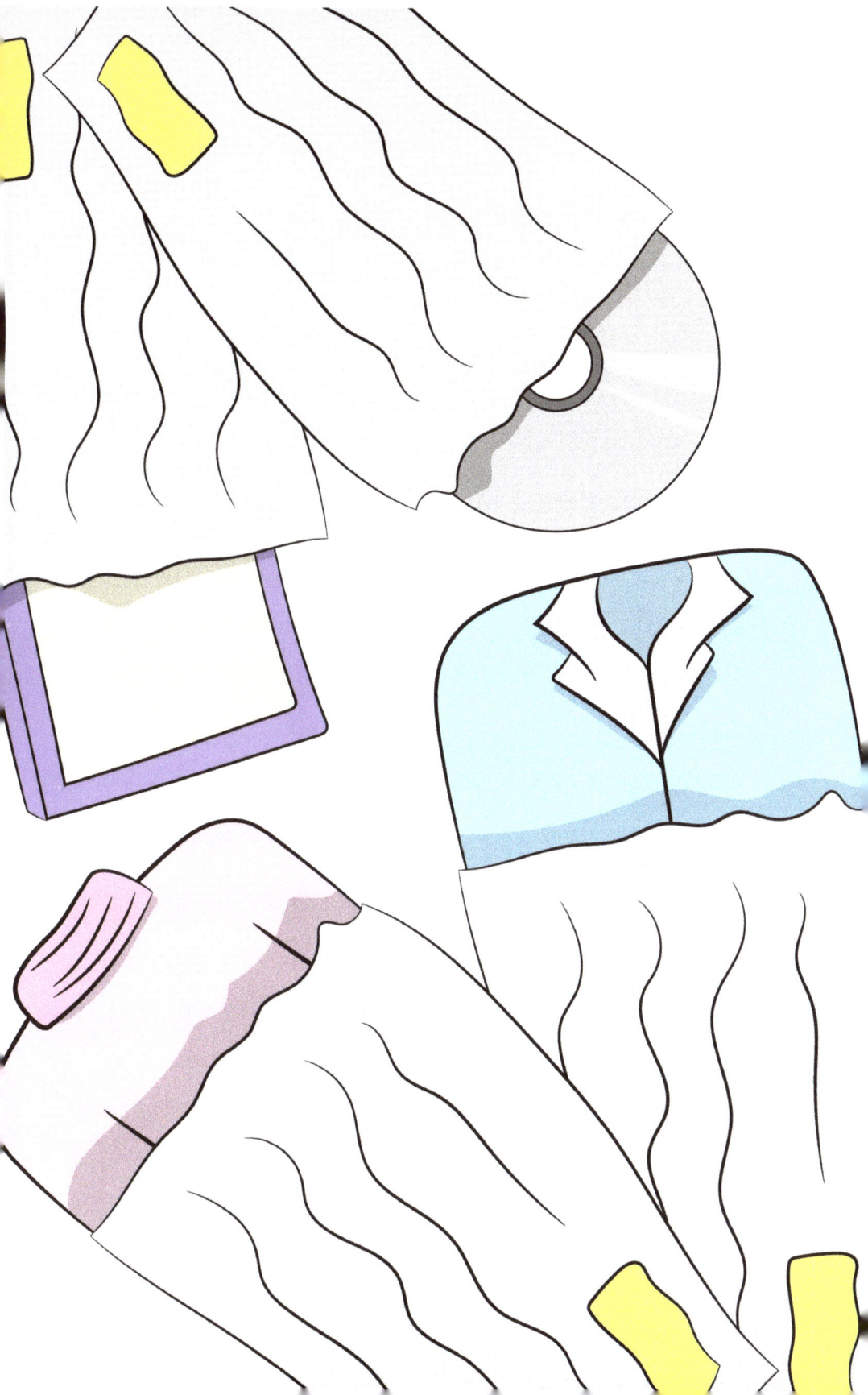

Anthony and Mia looked at the gifts.

"We haven't received anything," they said and started to cry. "Don't worry! Grandma Gil wouldn't forget about you," said Mom. "Yes," agreed Dad. "You know how much she loves you."

That made the children feel a bit better, but they were still worried. Why hadn't they received presents?

"I'm going to text Grandma to thank her," said Jillian. "So will I," added Joanna.

"And me," said Dominick.

"Where's my phone?" asked Deanna, looking around.

"Do you think that's a good idea?" asked Dad. "I know that she'd love to talk to you." "I'm too busy, Dad," said Deanna. "I have lots to do."

"And I have to go out and meet my friends," said Dominick.

"But think how happy she'd be if you called," suggested Mom. "But what about my friends," said Dominick.

"Which is more important?" asked Mom. "Saying thank you to Grandma or rushing off to see your friends?"

"You're right," said Dominick. "My friends will wait. Come on, let's call Grandma."

"Aren't you mad that Mom told you off?" Anthony whispered to Dominick.

"No," said Dominick. "Sometimes we need people to tell us if we're doing something wrong. I know my family loves me, even when they're a little cross with me."

Grandma Gil was thrilled to hear her grandchildren. She talked and laughed and then talked and laughed some more. Soon, a whole hour had gone by. At the end of the call, Grandma told the twins to expect a big surprise in the morning.

The next day, the twins were up early. Grandma had promised a big surprise, so they knew the mailman would be bringing presents. They jumped out of bed and rushed downstairs.

"Good morning, Mom," called Anthony. "Good morning, Dad," said Mia.

"Good morning, children," replied their parents.

As they ate breakfast, the twins kept looking at the door. After a while, there was a knock, and Mia ran to the door. It was the mailman! He handed Mia a small package and left. It was something for Dad.

THERE WERE NO PRESENTS!

Anthony smiled at Mia to try to cheer her up. Mia smiled back at Anthony to cheer him up.

They might not have presents, but they had each other… and Mom and Dad… and Dominick and Deanna and Jillian and Joanna. They had the best family in the world, and they knew how lucky they were…

Still, the presents were nice, so they were a little sad.

Just then, there was the sound of someone outside.

"I wonder who that could be?" said Dad, winking at the children. They jumped up and rushed to the door.

"Grandma!!" they yelled as they saw Grandma Gil climbing out of her motorhome. "Anthony! Mia! Come and give Grandma a hug!"

They led Grandma into the kitchen, and there were more hugs with the rest of the family.

Suddenly, Anthony remembered something.

"So, this is what Mom and Dad were planning the other morning."

"Yes," said Dad. "Grandma Gill has driven all the way from Florida to see us. This afternoon, we're all going camping in the mountains."

"Yes, and I've brought lots of toys for you both to take with you."

That night, the children sat next to a roaring campfire. Mom and Grandma Gil were laughing at one of Dad's jokes. Dominick and Deanna were singing together. Jillian and Joanna were lying on their backs, counting the stars.

"This is the best place in the world," said Mia.

"Yes," said Anthony… "Because we're with our family."

What have we learned?

- Family comes first.
- Your family will love you unconditionally.
- Think about what you can do for your family, not only what your family can do for you.
- Your family is your first line of defense. It's a safe place to share your concerns, fears and problems.

Now go make the world a better place!

www.ingramcontent.com/pod-product-compliance
Lightning Source LLC
LaVergne TN
LVHW072023060526
838200LV00058B/4658